S0-CKX-551

BLAIRSVILLE SENIOR HIGH SCHOOL
BLAIRSVILLE, PENNA.

FLYING SAFE?

BLAIRSVILLE SENIOR HIGH SCHOOL
BLAIRSVILLE, PENNA.

BY CHRISTOPHER LAMPTON

FLYING SAFE?

BLAIRSVILLE SENIOR HIGH SCHOOL
BLAIRSVILLE. PENNA.

FRANKLIN WATTS
NEW YORK/LONDON/TORONTO/SYDNEY/1986
AN IMPACT BOOK

Chart: © 1985 Time Inc. All rights reserved.

Photographs courtesy of: Smithsonian Institution: p. 5;
Culver Pictures, Inc.: p. 6; United Airlines: p. 9;
UPI/Bettman Newsphotos: pp. 12, 24, 25, 28, 35, 42, 52;
AP/Wide World: pp. 27, 69; Boeing Company: p. 59;
The Port Authority of N.Y. and N.J.: p. 60

Library of Congress Cataloging-in-Publication Data

Lampton, Christopher.
Flying safe?

(An Impact book)
Bibliography: p.
Includes index.
Summary: Surveys the history of air travel accidents and
safety, common causes of accidents, and methods for preventing
them and maximizing chances of survival after a crash.
1. Aeronautics—Safety measures—Juvenile literature.
2. Aeronautics—Accidents—Juvenile literature. [1. Aeronautics
—Accidents. 2. Aeronautics—Safety measures] I. Title.
TL553.5.L27 1986 363.1'24 85-31499
ISBN 0-531-10169-X

Copyright © 1986 by Christopher Lampton
All rights reserved
Printed in the United States of America
6 5 4 3 2 1

CONTENTS

BLAIRSVILLE SENIOR HIGH SCHOOL
BLAIRSVILLE, PENNA.

FLYING SAFE?

PREFACE

The year 1985 was the worst in civil aviation history. By late November, nearly 1,500 people had died in accidents involving regularly scheduled airlines, a grisly record that easily surpassed that of the previous worst year, 1974, when 1,299 persons were killed. More frightening still, the 1974 record had been surpassed by early August of 1985, when the year was barely more than half over, leaving frightened air travelers nearly five months to contemplate what horrifying new statistics the remainder of the year might bring.

And yet, paradoxically, flying remains one of the safest methods of transportation, far less dangerous than traveling by car. In the United States alone, more than 300 million passengers fly on scheduled airlines each year and, barring some unforeseen cataclysm, only the smallest fraction will ever be involved in any kind of airline accident. Fewer still will lose their lives.

Is flying safe? Statistically, yes, but that may not be the really important question. More to the point: Is flying as safe as it should be? To many observers, the answer is no. Relatively few people are killed in airline accidents each year, compared to the tens of thousands who die in automobile accidents in the United States alone, or the millions who die of cancer or heart attacks. But many of those who are killed may die unnecessarily, because of a sluggish bureaucracy that has been too slow to implement the advanced technology necessary to avoid many types of airline disasters, and because of corporations that may feel that saving lives is just plain too expensive.

This book is not intended as an indictment of the airline industry, or of the government agencies that regulate that industry. Rather, it is a look at the way in which airline accidents occur, and at some of the ways in which they can be prevented. And, before the book is over, we will look at the ways in which you, the reader, can maximize your own chances of surviving should you, against all odds, find yourself caught up in that most terrifying of man-made disasters: the airplane crash.

The first airplane flight in history ended in a crash.

On December 17, 1903, Wilbur and Orville Wright brought their *Wright Flyer*—history's first true airplane—to the barren dunes at Kitty Hawk, North Carolina, for its historic maiden flight. They yoked the plane to a 60-foot (18-m) guide rail, from which it could detach itself automatically once it gained sufficient speed. At 10:35 in the morning, Orville crawled on board the small plane and revved the engine, while Wilbur released the tether that held the machine secure in the strong winds that blew from nearby Cape Hatteras.

Later, Orville wrote:

The machine started very slowly. Wilbur was able to stay with it until it lifted from the track after a 40-foot [12-m] run.

The course of the flight up and down was exceedingly erratic, partly because of the gusty air, partly because of my inexperience in handling this machine. It would rise suddenly to about 10 feet [3 m], and then as suddenly . . . dart for the ground. On one of these darts it hit the ground. It had been in the air 12 seconds, and covered a distance of 120 feet [37 m].

The *Wright Flyer* was not hurt; neither was Orville. Undaunted, the brothers switched places and launched the *Flyer* again. At noon, in the final flight of the day, Wilbur piloted the tiny craft on a voyage of 852 feet (260 m) across the dunes.

The Age of Aviation had begun. The Age of Air Safety was still decades in the future.

The first fatal air crash occurred four years later. Once again, Orville Wright was at the helm. On September 17, 1907, the brothers were demonstrating one of their planes for the military. Orville took a passenger, Lieutenant Thomas E. Selfridge, on board for a short flight. One of the wires strung between the plane's twin wings broke in flight and became twisted in the propeller. The plane plunged to the ground. Selfridge was killed, and Orville badly injured.

In a very real way, there was no such thing as air safety in the early days of flight. A pilot took his life in his hands when he soared away from the security of the ground, and only skill and constant alertness brought him back in one piece. There was no such thing as a pilot's license; a pilot was anyone who had an airplane and the nerve to fly it. Learning to fly was something you did in the air, often all by yourself, and slow learners never finished the first lesson.

Aviation began to mature during World War I. When the war began, in Europe, airplanes were used entirely for reconnaissance—that is, for reporting the location of enemy troops. But by the end of the war they had become powerful fighting machines, armed with deadly

On December 17, 1903, at Kitty Hawk,
North Carolina, the age of aviation
began. With Orville Wright at the
controls, the Wright Flyer rises into
the air, as Wilbur watches.

When World War I ended in 1918, many former Army pilots became barnstormers. Commercial aviation was in its infancy, and flying was considered a novelty.

weapons and manned by pilots with finely honed combat skills.

When the war ended in 1918, a generation of pilots returned to civilian lives. In the United States, many of these pilots turned to barnstorming—traveling aerobatic exhibitions where flying daredevils could amaze audiences with feats of aerial bravado. The barnstormers provided many Americans with their first close look at what aviation was about—and many of those Americans were probably scared away from flying for the rest of their lives.

During the 1920s, however—at the same time as the barnstormers were touring their way across middle America—another, more enduring phenomenon began to emerge, first in Europe and then, to a lesser extent, in the United States: passenger flying. The airplane was the fastest method of transportation yet invented, and people in a hurry were willing to pay a lot of money to someone who could fly them to their destination. The early passenger flights were expensive—the early planes could hold no more than one or two passengers—and not particularly reliable, but there were always people who were willing to foot the bill and take the risk. Small airline companies sprang up around the world, most of them flying short flights between cities. In a gradual, haphazard way, commercial aviation was born.

By the 1930s, it had even become a big business. The United States, which had initially lagged behind Europe in the development of the aviation industry, was now its center. Most of the small airline companies vanished, either because they could no longer compete or because they were absorbed by larger companies, such as the newly formed United Airlines and Pan-American Airlines.

Commercial aviation as we know it today would never have been possible without the development of new technology, in the form of airplanes that were larger, faster, and more reliable than the craft of the teens and twenties.

The first of these modern passenger airplanes was the Boeing 247, built by Boeing Corporation, one of the three great airplane manufacturers of the last half century. (The other two are McDonnell-Douglas and Lockheed, names that will appear often in the pages that follow.) The 247 was powered by the sophisticated Wasp engine, manufactured by the Pratt and Whitney Company (another name that will recur in later chapters). It carried ten passengers and cruised at a speed of 160 miles an hour (257 kph).

The 247 was soon superseded by the Douglas DC-2 and later the DC-3, one of the most popular airplanes of all time. (As late as 1968, the DC-3 still outnumbered all other types of airplanes in use for air transport.) The DC-3 carried twenty-one passengers and flew 10 to 15 miles an hour (16–24 kph) faster than the 247. American Airlines, the airline company that sponsored the development of the DC-3, rapidly became one of the top airlines in the world, because it could transport more passengers than anyone else and it could get them where they were going, faster.

These Boeing and Douglas planes, along with the Lockheed Constellation, revolutionized the aviation industry. They were sturdily built, reliable—and safe, or reasonably so. Crashes happened, but the newly powerful aviation industry of the 1930s took its business seriously, and this meant taking steps to insure the safety of passengers. Toward that end, a new breed of college-educated, extensively trained pilots were brought in to replace the barnstormers who had been with the industry from its start. Electronic instruments, including radios, were put into planes so that the pilot could be kept constantly aware of conditions around the plane and on the ground.

But the efforts of the airlines were not enough. As more and more planes took to the skies, it was inevitable that more and more accidents would occur—and occur

*The first standard passenger plane
was the Boeing 247.*

they did. It became increasingly obvious that strict laws were needed to regulate the activities of pilots and airliners, to keep the airways from degenerating into chaos. By the mid-1930s, several government agencies shared among themselves the responsibility for regulating the airlines—most of the safety-related regulation came out of the Bureau of Air Commerce—but these agencies were small and understaffed and woefully inadequate to the task of monitoring the burgeoning airline industry.

Finally, in the late 1930s, the U.S. government—rather belatedly—moved to provide effective regulation for the airlines. Unfortunately, as is so often the case with government regulation, someone had to die before steps were taken to make the heavens safe.

May 5, 1935. The proverbial dark and stormy night. Captain Harvey Bolton of TWA took off in a Douglas DC-2 from the airport at Albuquerque, New Mexico, on the second leg of a long flight from Los Angeles, California, to Newark, New Jersey, with nine passengers aboard. The trip was a bad one almost from the start. As storm clouds moved in, Bolton became aware that his radio was no longer functioning properly; he could still receive messages from ground stations, but could not broadcast messages of his own.

Lost in the rapidly thickening clouds, unable to radio for help, Bolton wandered desperately in hopes of picking up a radio signal from an emergency landing field. Flying just above the treetops in an attempt to escape the low-hanging clouds and mist, Bolton accidentally guided his plane into a ravine. At the end of the ravine, he was unable to pull the plane up in time, and he crashed.

Surprisingly, only five people were killed in the crash, three of the passengers plus Captain Bolton and his co-pilot. Six passengers survived. The incident might have been just another minor harrowing statistic in the history of aviation, had it not been for a quirk of fate: one of the passengers who died was a United States senator.

And not just any senator: Bronson Cutting was one of the most revered men in Congress. Grieved and infuriated by his death, his colleagues in Washington ordered a congressional inquiry into the crash. Why, they asked, was the plane allowed to take off with a faulty radio? Why was the flight not routed away from the bad weather, to an alternate field? And why didn't Bolton land as soon as he became aware that the radio was defective?

The conclusion, reached at painful length, was that the government needed an effective means of policing the aviation industry. Under the administration of President Franklin D. Roosevelt, who was first elected to office in the depression year of 1932, airline regulation—such as it was—had been spread out through a large number of relatively ineffectual government agencies. Congress, in response to the Cutting Crash (as it was now called), demanded that a new agency be formed and given broad powers to supervise the safety of the airways.

In 1938, the Civil Aeronautics Act was passed. As amended by President Roosevelt two years later, the Act created a pair of governmental bodies that, between them, were responsible for air safety (and other aspects of commercial aviation) in this country. One of these bodies, the Civil Aeronautics Administration (CAA), had regulatory authority over all safety-related aspects of American aviation; the other body, the Civil Aeronautics Board (CAB), had authority to investigate airplane accidents and make recommendations concerning air safety, but no actual legal authority to enforce its wishes in these areas.

In essence, this was the beginning of modern air safety. So successful were the CAA and CAB at tightening the safety standards of the airlines that, in the year 1940, not a single life was lost in an accident involving a United

States airline. But commercial aviation was still relatively young in 1940, and as the skies became increasingly crowded and the planes faster and more packed with passengers, true safety of the airways became more and more difficult to achieve.

Today, air safety in the United States is supervised by the Federal Aviation Administration (FAA), a wing of the Department of Transportation and successor to the CAA. The FAA is a large and powerful agency, with local bureaus spread across the United States as well as in other countries, and its control over almost all safety-related aspects of American aviation is absolute.

The mandate of the agency is impressive. It controls the routes that planes take through the skies, the airworthiness of new aircraft, the construction of airports, the maintenance of air navigation installations, and many other aspects of aviation. Its most powerful tool is the Airworthiness Directive, or AD. With the AD, the FAA can ground entire fleets of airplanes, if it so much as suspects that they may be unsafe.

As we shall see later in this book, the FAA has come in for a large share of criticism for the way in which it has looked out for the safety of the airways over the past quarter of a century, and especially for its use of—or failure to use—the Airworthiness Directive. Some of the crit-

Senator Bronson Cutting of New Mexico, in January 1935, three months before he was killed in an airplane crash. His death led to the passage of the Civil Aeronautics Act and the beginning of modern air safety.

icism has come from a second government body: the National Transportation Safety Board (NTSB).

Created from an arm of the old Civil Aeronautics Board, the NTSB was at one time part of the Department of Transportation, but in 1974 Congress made it into an independent entity. The NTSB exists for one purpose: to determine the cause of transportation accidents and to find ways in which they can be avoided. Although it has jurisdiction over several forms of transportation accidents, including highway, marine, and railroad accidents, the NTSB investigates *all* commercial aviation accidents.

One of its tools in these investigations is the Go Team, a group of NTSB investigators rapidly assembled whenever a major transportation accident occurs and transported immediately to the site. The members of the Go Team are chosen from a number of specialties. According to the NTSB's 1984 Annual Report to Congress:

> A typical aviation Go Team could include an air traffic control specialist, a meteorologist, a human performance expert, an expert trained in witness interrogation, an engine specialist as well as experts in hydraulics, and electrical systems/maintenance/records.

The Go Team, in short, is chosen for wide-ranging expertise. The findings of the Go Team, and of the NTSB investigators in general, are widely respected in the industry, because the investigators are often themselves pilots, and possess considerable knowledge of aviation, and aviation-related subjects. The NTSB can be quite outspoken in its recommendations. Alas, like the old CAB from which it was formed, it has no power to enforce these recommendations; that is the job of the FAA. And on more than a few occasions the FAA has chosen to ignore the NTSB's advice.

The relation between the NTSB and the FAA is therefore a volatile one. Conflicts arise frequently between the two bodies, as we shall see.

Perhaps the best-known weapon in the aviation accident investigator's arsenal is the so-called black box (the box is actually orange)—the recording system that keeps a detailed record of the final moments of an ill-fated flight.

Most large airplanes carry two different kinds of flight recorder. One records the voices of the crew in the cockpit, along with the radio transmissions between the airplane and traffic controllers on the ground. The second records, in electronic form, detailed information about the flight itself: the time, altitude, and speed at which the airplane is flying, its compass heading, vertical acceleration, and physical orientation. Generally the flight recorders are placed in the rear of the airplane, so that they will receive relatively little damage in the event of collision.

When investigators arrive at the scene of the air crash, one of the first things they do is to remove the black box and put it into safekeeping. The flight recorder holds deep and often terrifying secrets about why a plane crashes, and what can be done to keep future flights from crashing in the same way.

CHAPTER TWO
RUSH HOUR IN THE SKY

The most common automobile accident is the "fender bender"—a minor collision that puts a small dent in the chrome of one or both cars involved. Although a fender bender may result in hot tempers, traffic tie-ups, and inflated repair costs, it rarely results in loss of life or even major injury.

Fender benders happen, in large part, because highways are crowded, and collisions between cars are inevitable unless extraordinary precautions are taken to avoid them.

The skies can get crowded, too—especially around airports. But there is no such thing as a fender bender in the sky. If two airplanes collide while in the air—or even while on the ground—it is *always* a major accident. It is therefore necessary that extraordinary precautions be taken to keep such collisions from happening.

The extraordinary precaution that is taken to prevent so-called mid-air collisions is the air traffic control system, probably the most important single aspect of air safety in the United States, or anywhere.

By the mid-1920s, the skies of the United States were divided up into air routes, imaginary highways that stretched from one city to another, providing paths along which pilots could fly from airport to airport.

The key to this early air route system was the radio beam, a radio signal broadcast continually from certain major airports that a pilot could receive on his cockpit radio. By the sound of the radio signal, the pilot could tell if he was heading directly toward the airport, or flying off at a tangent to it. By "flying the beam," a pilot could find his way unerringly across the trackless wildernesses of the United States, even in the middle of the night or in bad weather (though the beam signals were sometimes disrupted by static during storms).

At the airports themselves, flashing beacons were placed on the ground or atop towers to guide the pilot to a landing once the plane was in visual range of the airport.

In addition to these beacons and radio beams, most major airports had some sort of traffic control system to keep the airways directly above the airport from becoming dangerously crowded with planes. At first, this traffic control consisted chiefly of workers who stood on the airfield and flashed lights at airplane pilots, telling them when it was safe to take off or land. By the 1930s, however, the flashing lights began to be supplemented by radio control, with pilots in their planes talking directly to controllers at the airport, who guided the pilots to safe landings, making sure that no two planes ever tried to land in the same place at the same time.

The people who guided the planes are called air traffic controllers, and what they did (and still do) is called air traffic control, or ATC for short.

After World War II, in the mid-1940s, the air traffic controller gained a powerful new tool—radar. A radar beam scanning the skies around an airport provided the air traffic controller with a visual image, on a televisionlike monitor, of all airplanes in the vicinity, and their relative positions. If two planes were flying too close to one another, the controller could see this on the radar screen and warn the planes to move further apart. By the 1950s, all major airports had radar systems that could monitor the positions of airplanes in their vicinity.

Obviously, airports were the place where air traffic control was needed the most, because that was where the skies were the most crowded and where accidental collisions between planes were most likely to occur.

The airspace between airports was another matter. A pilot flying the vast open spaces between airports was more or less on his or her own recognizance. In the 1930s and '40s, en route air traffic control centers began to be established between airports, but these were little more than radio checkpoints which could give the pilot information about weather conditions and the locations of other airplanes. The controllers in these en route centers would attempt to keep track of the whereabouts of each plane in their vicinity, but this information was based largely on sporadic radio contact with the planes, and was usually out of date minutes after it was received. Without radar, the en route controller could only monitor the relative positions of planes by moving small markers across large maps, and watching to see if any two markers came close enough to endanger the planes that they represented.

In those days—until roughly thirty years ago—it was the pilot's responsibility to avoid midair collisions while en route between airports. The collision-avoidance system practiced by the pilots was called "see and be seen"— that is, each pilot kept an eye out for other planes and depended on the pilots of those other planes to do the same.

"See and be seen" was an integral part of the early air safety system, but it had profound disadvantages. As planes were built that could fly at higher and higher speeds, pilots had commensurately less time to spot other planes that may have wandered into their paths. At the speeds at which a typical passenger airliner flew in the mid-1950s, a pilot might have no more than a few seconds to avoid colliding with another plane after it came into view, barely enough time to change the course of the plane. And that was under ideal visual conditions. On a cloudy day, or in the dark of night, the pilot might have less than a second.

By 1956, it became obvious that, unless something were done and done soon, a major airline collision was inevitable. That was a horrifying prospect indeed. So, the Civil Aeronautics Administration began to draw up a five-year plan that would revolutionize the nation's air traffic control system, placing radar beacons in en route centers and putting large airplanes completely under the control of the air traffic controllers. Like traffic cops of the air, the controllers would keep all airplanes sufficiently separated from each other in the sky so that collisions simply could not happen.

But, like any underfunded bureaucratic body, the CAA moved with glacial slowness, and before it could even finish drawing up its plan, the horrifying prospect became horrifyingly real.

June 30, 1956. Two airliners—a TWA Superconstellation (Lockheed's successor to the Constellation) and a United DC-7—flew out of Los Angeles International Airport within three minutes of one another, both headed east. The TWA was on its way to Kansas City, the United to Chicago. Because they were going to different destinations, each plane was to follow a different route. However, the two routes crossed at one point: directly over the Grand Canyon.

This didn't present a problem, because the two planes were flying at slightly different speeds and at different altitudes. Thus, they would arrive at the Grand Canyon at different times, and even if by some accident they arrived at the Canyon simultaneously, one would simply fly over the other. And even if, by the wildest of coincidences, the two planes crossed the Canyon at the same time and at the same altitude, the planes would be flying in clear air, high above the clouds, and the two pilots would surely be able to see one another in time to avoid any collision.

In short, the likelihood that the two planes would run into one another was so small that such an accident could reasonably be called "impossible"; it would involve a string of coincidences much too incredible to contemplate.

And yet, one by one, the coincidences happened. Somehow the TWA moved to the same cruising level as the United, despite the effort of en route controllers to keep them at different altitudes. At 9:59 A.M., when the pilots of the two aircraft reported their estimated time of arrival at the Grand Canyon to their respective controllers, both gave an arrival time of 10:31. And the clear sky above the cloud tops gave way to soaring thunderheads; both pilots apparently found their airplanes passing through a cloud—just before they arrived at the Grand Canyon.

The "impossible" accident happened. Apparently, the two planes flew out of the cloud bank at the same moment. Whether or not they saw one another before the collision is hard to say; no one survived to tell the story. The wing of the DC-7 hit the rudder of the Superconstellation, then the bodies of the two planes collided. The Superconstellation was ripped apart; the DC-7 lost a wing. Both plunged to the ground, within 1½ miles (2.4 km) of each other, at the bottom of the Grand Canyon.

At the Salt Lake en route center, a controller heard the final message from the DC-7: "Salt Lake, United 718 . . . ah . . . we're going in."

The accident happened at exactly 10:31; the planes were precisely on schedule. One hundred twenty-eight people were killed.

No United States senator was aboard the airplanes that collided over the Grand Canyon, but the sheer horror of 128 individuals dying in what was then the worst aviation accident of all time galvanized the government into action, much as the Cutting Crash had done two decades earlier. Congress approved the CAA's five-year plan—changing it in the process to a three-year plan—and appropriated handsome sums of money to install radar at en route centers and modernize the nation's navigation system. Then, in 1958, they passed the Federal Aviation Act, abolishing the CAA altogether and replacing it with the Federal Aviation Agency, which later became the Federal Aviation Administration.

The improvements were badly needed; no one questioned that. But even as the CAA and FAA were accelerating the technology of air traffic control, the manufacturers of airplanes were giving those airplanes greater capabilities, which made them more difficult for air controllers to keep track of.

In 1956, Boeing introduced a new model of airplane: the Boeing 707, the first U.S. passenger jet. While earlier planes had lumbered along on now-primitive propeller power, the jets shot into the sky on powerful jets of air. They moved twice as fast as the earlier planes, and flew even higher.

The "see and be seen" system of collision avoidance became obsolete with the introduction of the passenger jet. Now airplane pilots would have no time at all to react in the face of an imminent collision. In fact, jets moved so quickly that even air traffic controllers armed with radar had difficulty keeping planes separated in the sky.

The first midair collision involving a passenger jet took place only four years after the Grand Canyon crash, on

December 16, 1960. And it occurred over a landscape that was every bit as impressive: downtown New York City.

Once again, the planes involved were from United and TWA—a DC-8 and a Super-Constellation, respectively. The only difference, in fact, between the participants in this crash and the one over the Grand Canyon was that the United aircraft was a DC-8 rather than a DC-7. This was a significant difference, however, because the DC-8, unlike the DC-7, is a jet.

The Constellation was headed toward La Guardia Airport, just outside of Manhattan; the DC-8 was circling through the skies, waiting for permission to land at nearby Idlewild (later renamed Kennedy) airport. Apparently the navigational equipment on board the DC-8 was defective, because the pilot wandered off the path in which the air traffic controller had placed him and into the path taken by the Constellation. The controller at La Guardia tried to warn the TWA plane: "Jet traffic on your right now at 3 o'clock at 1 mile [1.6 km]." The pilot heard the message and responded, but he couldn't see the jet. The controller ordered him to veer left, but it was too late. The jet, closing the distance between the two planes at a speed that would have been unimaginable only a few years earlier, intercepted the path of the TWA plane, and they both fell to earth.

The jet smashed into a row of houses in Brooklyn; the Constellation, which managed to remain in the air a few seconds longer, crashed several miles away, on Staten Island. All of the passengers on the jet were killed. But, surprisingly, one of the passengers aboard the Constellation—an eleven-year-old boy named Stephen Baltz—survived, tossed from the wreckage into a nearby bank of snow. He was badly burned, however, and sadly, he died a few days later.

The nation was shocked by the crash, but there was little that could be done to prevent a sequel, except wait with crossed fingers for the government to bring the air traffic control system into the jet age, as it was desperately struggling to do. In some ways, the situation the aviation community was faced with in 1960 symbolizes the history of aviation in general: a race between the technology of flight and the technology of air safety to prevent the skies from degenerating into total chaos. So far, the technology of air safety seems to be winning, but occasionally, as in 1956 and in 1960—and again in 1985—we are reminded that the race is a close one.

The modern U.S. air traffic control system, born out of such incidents as those described above, is a sophisticated one. Although it has its critics, it seems to work about as well as anyone could expect it to, at least so far. Collisions still happen—most notably a catastrophic collision between a small private plane and a Pacific Southwest Airlines Boeing 727 at Lindbergh Field in San Diego in 1979—but they are thankfully few and far between.

Today, the United States is crisscrossed with hundreds of thousands of miles of air routes, the invisible highways in the sky that pilots follow between airports. The controllers at twenty-one en route air traffic control centers guide the planes along these air routes with radar and radio. Each air route, however, is divided by altitude into two sections, one for jets and another for smaller, slower planes. Jets are usually placed by controllers at cruising altitudes of more than 18,000 feet (549 m); other planes are kept lower. Jets are kept under positive control at all times—that is, from the moment a jet enters the jurisdiction of an en route center, a controller at that center monitors the craft's every movement, and the pilot cannot change altitude, speed, or direction without the controller's permission. When the jet leaves the center's jurisdiction, or enters the vicinity of its destination airport, the controller "hands it off" to a controller in the next center along the plane's path or at the airport. The goal of the

The first midair collision involving a jet
occurred over New York City in 1960 when
a United Airlines DC-8 and a TWA Constellation
collided. Left: fire fighters work to control
the blaze after the DC-8 fell into a residential
area of Brooklyn. Above: the remains of the
Constellation, which crashed in Staten Island.

air traffic controller is to achieve separation—that is, to prevent the airplane under his or her charge from coming within a certain minimum distance of any other airplanes. Generally, a horizontal separation of 5 miles (8 km) is desirable, and an altitude separation of 1,000 to 2,000 feet (304–610 m). As long as separation is achieved, collisions are unable to happen.

In the air traffic control centers, each controller sits in front of a radar screen not unlike those in use since the 1940s. The modern radar image, however, is computer augmented; most large airplanes, and many smaller airplanes, are depicted as visible blips surrounded by numbers, representing the airplane's location, altitude, speed, direction, and identification code. This information is supplied by a device called a transponder on board the airplane itself, which broadcasts a continually updated signal to the air traffic center; this signal is converted by the air traffic computers into the numbers seen on the controller's screen.

As sophisticated as this air traffic control system is, it has its critics—and the criticism was greatly exacerbated by an event that occurred in 1981. The air controller's union—the Professional Air Traffic Controllers' Organization, or PATCO—went on strike, demanding higher pay and improved working conditions. Because of the vital role that the air controllers play in modern aviation, the strike paralyzed air commerce in the United States. However, air traffic controllers are government employees—they work, in fact, for the FAA—and government employees do not have the legal right to strike, no matter how valid they feel their grievances to be.

President Ronald Reagan, the head of the government for which the PATCO members worked, requested that the controllers come back to their jobs; when only a few complied with his request, he took the almost unprec-

*Air traffic controllers in training learn the basics
of radar in this terminal approach control laboratory.
This course can simulate conditions approximating
a busy high-density airport.*

edented step of firing all of the controllers who remained on strike, 11,500 of them in all.

Needless to say, the union members and those who had supported them in their strike were furious, but the majority of Americans felt that the president had made the proper response. Backed by this public mandate, Reagan ordered the FAA to replace the fired controllers with military air controllers and trainees. Critics of the FAA, as well as PATCO officials, warned that the results would be disastrous. Air traffic control is a job requiring finely honed skills, and the new controllers, with their considerably reduced numbers, would be unable to cope with the complexities and tensions of modern aviation. Inevitably, there would be midair collisions.

Perhaps surprisingly, this has not turned out to be the case. There have been no midair collisions in the United States since the striking air traffic controllers were fired, and relatively few accidents in which air traffic control problems were implicated.

On the other hand, according to some reports, the number of near collisions has increased. On January 1, 1984—New Year's Day—a DC-10 and a Boeing 747, both from Pan American Airways, passed within 300 feet (91 m) of one another as they flew over the Atlantic Ocean near Miami. According to the National Transportation

When striking air traffic controllers were fired by President Reagan in 1981 and replaced by military air controllers and inexperienced trainees, some people believed that there would be an increase in airplane accidents.

Safety Board team that investigated the incident, an actual collision may have been avoided only because the pilot of the DC-10 pulled his plane out of the way seconds before the disaster would have occurred—the old "see and be seen" technique in action, decades after it should have become unnecessary.

September 1984 seems to have been an especially bad month for near misses in the sky. On September 7 in Arizona a jet passed within 500 feet (152 m) of a small plane near Phoenix Airport. On September 12 another jet nearly collided with a cargo plane 80 miles (129 km) from San Juan, Puerto Rico. And, on September 30, an Air Force plane came within three-quarters of a mile (1.2 km)—still an unacceptably small separation—of a private plane, an incident that would seem relatively unremarkable except that one of the passengers on the Air Force plane was Vice-President George Bush.

On September 24, 1985, an especially harrowing incident occurred at National Airport in Washington, D.C., when an Eastern Airlines jet was forced to abort its takeoff near the end of the runway to avoid colliding with a helicopter, which had apparently been given clearance to take off directly across the path of the Eastern craft. The jet nearly plunged into the Potomac River—and *would* have plunged into the river if the accident had occurred a few years earlier, before the runway had been lengthened.

As if these stories weren't frightening enough, many aviation critics, such as John Galipault of the Aviation Safety Institute, claim that the vast majority of near collisions are never even reported. According to Galipault, "Controllers and pilots are not reporting them if they can avoid it; it's a lot of hassle."

With all of these reported and unreported near misses, is another major collision in the offing? We can certainly hope not. The fledgling air traffic controllers of 1981 are now seasoned professionals. The number of controllers monitoring the nation's skies is practically, though not quite, up to its prestrike level, and Transportation Secretary Elizabeth Dole promised in September of 1985 to hire one thousand more controllers by 1987.

Other critics of the air traffic control system have long claimed that the equipment used by the controllers is outdated and should be replaced and modernized. Apparently, the FAA agrees. At about the time of the PATCO strike the agency launched a major modernization program, to bring the technology used by the controllers up to the state-of-the-art. The program is called the National Airspace System, and it has been estimated that it will take ten to fifteen billion dollars—and about ten years—to reach fruition.

For the most part, this modernization program involves passing much of the work now done by air traffic controllers to computers. For instance, computers will do most of the flight path calculations now done by human controllers, and computers will monitor weather conditions in the vicinity of the center. Further, the computers at the ground stations will be able to talk directly with computers on board the airplanes, eliminating much of the confusing human-to-human chatter that now clogs the airwaves around airport and en route centers.

But human beings will never be removed entirely from the system. The idea behind the National Airspace System is that computers will augment the work of human controllers, so that a smaller number of controllers will be needed to control a larger number of airplanes.

As usually seems to be the case, the new system is arriving in the nick of time. It is estimated that by the end of the century the number of airplanes in U.S. skies could easily increase by 50 percent—and perhaps even double.

The technology of air safety will have to move awfully fast to win this race!

CHAPTER THREE
A WING AND A PRAYER

The first explosion occurred less than fifteen minutes after Japan Air Lines (JAL) flight 123 left Haneda Airport, near Tokyo, on the evening of August 12, 1985. The plane, a wide-bodied Boeing 747 jumbo jet, was packed with 524 people, most on their way to visit families for a celebration of the Japanese holiday, Bon.

An off-duty flight attendant, Yumi Ochiai, seated in the rear of the passenger cabin, heard a sharp noise over-head, loud enough to hurt her ears. The cabin filled with white mist as thin, cold air outside the plane flooded into the warm cabin. Emergency oxygen masks dropped automatically from the ceiling, to provide passengers with air.

Something had gone wrong. Flight 123 was in trouble.

In the cockpit Captain Masami Takahama, a skilled pilot who had been with the airline for nearly two decades, had no idea what the problem was. All he knew was that he could no longer steer his plane. An air traffic controller in Tokyo radioed to tell him that the plane was going in the wrong direction, northwest instead of east, away from the airport where he was scheduled to land. Takahama radioed back, in English: "Uncontrol!" He could not control his airplane.

Desperately, Takahama tried to steer his plane back to Haneda by applying power alternately to his left and right engines. The effect was to roll the plane violently from side to side. A witness on the ground later described the wobbling progress that the plane made through the skies: "It was flying just like a wobbling drunk."

To some extent, Takahama's maneuver was successful. The plane turned back toward Haneda—and kept right on turning. The plane spun through a full 360 degrees, until it was heading in the wrong direction again.

Back in the passenger cabin, flight attendant Ochiai had become aware that the air in the cabin was breathable without special oxygen masks, and had begun to instruct the passengers in emergency procedures, showing them how to brace in their seats in the event of a crash and helping them don life preservers.

By some miracle, the skilled Captain Takahama managed to keep the plane in the air for more than half an hour after the initial explosion—whatever it was—had rendered the craft unsteerable. Some passengers, aware that they might be on the verge of death, took the time to write messages to loved ones back home. The words of one passenger, found later among his belongings, probably summed up the feelings of all on board: "I don't want to take any more planes. Please, Lord, help me."

At roughly 6:45 P.M., twenty minutes after the mysterious explosion, the 747 began to lose altitude. For another ten minutes it seemed to bob up and down, losing and gaining altitude as the crew apparently fought to keep it aloft. Then it plunged. "The plane started dropping at a sharp angle," said Ochiai later. "Almost vertically."

Somehow the craft had wandered into a mountainous

region of Japan, and at 6:57 P.M., at a height of 4,700 feet (1,433 m), it rammed into the slope of Mount Osutaka. Wreckage was strewn all along the slope, much of it burning.

So remote was the area where Flight 123 crashed that rescuers were unable to reach the site until the next morning. When they got there they found that, against the odds, four people had managed to survive, including flight attendant Ochiai. But 520 people were dead, making the crash of JAL 123 the worst single-plane accident in aviation history.

What went wrong? The precise cause of the accident was difficult to determine, but the broad outlines were clear: the plane had lost its tail section, including the tail fin, which keeps the plane stable in flight, and the rudder, which allows the pilot to steer. Flight 123 was indeed uncontrollable. Under the circumstances, it was remarkable that it had managed to stay in the air as long as it had.

And why was the tail fin lost? That's more difficult to say. JAL 123 was not a new airplane; it had been put into service eleven years earlier, in 1974. And it had a history of accidents. Twice, in 1978, it had undergone "hard landings"; once, it had dragged its tail section across a landing field at more than 120 mph (193 kph), injuring passengers and knocking several panels off the tail. Boeing had repaired the tail section, declaring it as good as new, but the repair could nonetheless have been faulty. Even if it was, though, it may not have contributed to the crash.

The explosion heard by Ochiai and the white mist observed immediately after indicate that the plane underwent explosive decompression, with the highly pressurized air inside the cabin escaping and being replaced by the thinner air outside the plane. If the air had escaped violently toward the rear of the plane, it might have helped to shear away the tail section, especially if the tail section

When Japan Air Lines flight 123 crashed on August 12, 1985, rescue efforts were hampered by the remoteness of the site and the rugged terrain. Only 4 of the 524 people survived the crash.

had been weakened by earlier accidents. But what could have caused this decompression? No one knows. A bomb has been suggested, but there is no evidence that this is the case.

Disturbed by the possibility that the accident may have been caused by a flaw in their jet, the Boeing Corporation suggested that all airlines using 747s should inspect the tail section of their planes. In Japan, when such an inspection was performed following the crash of Flight 123, more than half of the nation's fleet of 747s proved to have "abnormalities" in their tail sections, ranging from broken bolts, to cracks and scratches, to rusty bearings.

This accident, and several others that have occurred in recent years, is a reminder of a simple, but worrisome, truth: an airplane is a machine, and machines sometimes fall apart.

An airplane is not just a machine, though: it is a precision machine, like a Swiss watch. It is made up of hundreds of thousands of parts, which must work together in near perfect coordination if the craft is to perform its function properly.

The most important single part of the plane is not the engine or the electronic guidance system, or even the pilot—though all of these parts are of extreme importance. The most important single part of an airplane is, in fact, its shape.

The shape of an airplane is not designed with an eye toward making it look pretty, or impressive, or even to make it fit snugly in a hangar. It is designed according to certain aerodynamic principles: the shape of an airplane is what makes it fly.

The body of an airplane (in particular the wings of the plane) is constructed in such a way that when air flows past it at a high speed, a phenonemon called lift will occur. When lift occurs, the suction of the air rushing past the wing literally pulls the plane upward—and flight is achieved.

At the same time as lift is occurring, a second phenomenon also occurs: drag. This is the suction of the air from behind the plane, pulling it backward. Drag is an undesirable effect, because it slows the movement of the plane through the air and reduces lift.

Thus, the shape of an airplane is intended to maximize lift and minimize drag.

However, the pilot of the plane is given a certain amount of control over these phenomena through the use of movable portions of the airplane's body, namely: ailerons, flaps, slats, and spoilers on the wings; elevators on the horizontal tail; and a rudder on the vertical tail. By manipulating these instruments, the pilot can cause minute changes in the shape of the plane, selectively increasing or decreasing the amount of drag and lift and thereby speeding the plane up or slowing it down, increasing the plane's altitude or bringing it back toward the earth.

We should note here an important aerodynamic fact that will have significance later in this book: the ability of an airplane to produce lift is entirely dependent on its speed relative to the air around it, which is called the airspeed of the plane, rather than its speed relative to the ground, or ground speed. Thus, an airplane moving at 50 mph (80 kph) relative to the ground and flying into a 50 mph headwind (i.e., a wind blowing opposite the direction in which the craft is moving) is actually moving at 100 mph relative to the air—the combined speed of its motion relative to the ground and the motion of the air itself. On the other hand, an airplane moving at 50 mph relative to the ground with a 50 mph tailwind (i.e., a wind blowing in the same direction the craft is moving) is actually moving at 0 mph relative to the air—and will stall, and fall right out of the sky, if it is aloft at the time. This is why airplanes always take off into the wind rather than with the wind. More on this general subject in the next chapter.

The engines of the airplane exist primarily to increase the forward movement of the craft through the air, so that lift can take place. On older airliners, and most smaller planes, the engines turn one or more propellers, which pull the aircraft forward through the air in much the same way the propeller on a boat pushes the boat forward through the water. On modern jetliners, the engine powers a stream of hot air that pushes the plane forward like a rocket.

All large airplanes have more than one engine, though where these engines are placed varies from one type of plane to another. Some have the engines on the wings, some in the rear, some in both places. Though it may surprise you to hear it, a plane can fly fairly well without all of its engines working, though it may become harder to steer. Of course, if a plane loses an engine, or if the pilot is forced to turn off an engine for safety reasons, the airplane is required to land immediately, at the nearest available airport. The loss of an engine in this manner is a more common incident that most people are aware; roughly one out of every 10,000 flights is aborted for just this reason. This may not seem like very much, until you consider that 14,000 passenger flights leave U.S. airports every day, making such incidents a daily occurrence in this country alone!

For airplanes that fly at very high altitudes—which is to say, all passenger jets—another part of the aircraft structure becomes important: the pressurized cabin. This is the portion of the plane where human beings reside, be they passengers or crew. Because the air at high altitudes is very thin and just about unbreathable, an extra supply of air must be kept inside the aircraft and it must be maintained under high pressure within the cabin, so that it will not thin out to the consistency of the air outside the plane. Naturally, this means that the cabin must be airtight, so that the pressurized air will not escape, like air from a punctured balloon. It it does escape, the result can be explosive, as in the sudden depressurization of JAL 123. Under extreme conditions, passengers can be sucked from the airplane in the violent outrush of air.

Obviously, if an airplane is indeed a precision instrument, it is important to maintain its structural integrity; airplanes should not be allowed to fall apart if it can be at all prevented. To this end, the FAA requires newly designed airplanes to pass a rigorous inspection process before they are allowed to carry passengers. And airplanes that have already been okayed for flight must be periodically inspected.

The airlines themselves, as well as the airplane manufacturers, have set up maintenance and inspection systems that meet and quite often exceed the FAA's requirements. On major airlines, certain airplane components are inspected after every flight; other components are inspected on a more irregular basis. Before each flight, a mechanic performs a "walk-around" of the plane, visually inspecting the machine to see if anything looks suspicious.

And yet airplanes, like Flight 123, still fall apart. Why? Is it a failure of the FAA inspection system, as some critics allege? Are the airlines and the manufacturers not always meeting their own high standards of maintenance? Or is it just the perversity of inanimate objects?

The answer may be: all of the above. Perhaps the most telling incident, or series of incidents, in the saga of airplane structural problems is the story of the McDonnell-Douglas DC-10, one of the most trouble-prone aircraft in the history of commercial aviation.

The DC-10 is a jumbo, or wide-bodied, jet. The jumbo jets are the largest passenger planes in existence, designed to hold from 300 to more than 500 passengers. The first DC-10 was put into service in 1971, shortly after two rivals of the McDonnell-Douglas Corporation had produced their own jumbo jets: the Boeing 747 and the Lockheed L-1011. It was no coincidence, of course, that the three major airplane manufacturers had all produced their first jumbo jets within a period of about two years. Airplane manufacture is a competitive business, and no corporation dares let a competitor hold a technological edge over it for very long.

American and United airlines both took delivery of brand-new DC-10s the year that it was introduced. Although it was a new plane, there was little worry about putting it into service. After all, it had just finished a lengthy process of testing and certification. Certainly it had proved its reliability.

A year later, on June 12, 1972, the troubles began.

At shortly after 9 o'clock that evening, an American Airlines DC-10 was flying east above Ontario, Canada, on its way from Detroit, Michigan, to Buffalo, New York. An explosion echoed through the craft and the passenger cabin began to depressurize, much as in the case of JAL 123.

The pilot, Captain Bryce McCormick, quickly became aware that he no longer was able to operate his rudder. The plane veered sharply to the right. Fighting to control the plane, he managed to turn back toward Detroit Metropolitan Airport, where he knew emergency equipment would be waiting for him on landing.

He made it to the airport. Because he was unable to guide the plane properly once it was on the ground, the DC-10 coasted across the field and into the grass beyond. An emergency team arrived seconds later and evacuated the passengers. No one was seriously injured.

Why had the pilot lost control of his plane? What had caused the cabin to depressurize?

The team from the National Transportation Safety Board arrived almost immediately, looking for answers to those and other questions.

The answer that they found held ominous implications. The cargo door had broken loose from the airplane shortly after the flight had begun. The door itself was found on an Ontario farm, along with—bizarrely enough—a wooden coffin containing the body of an elderly woman, which had apparently fallen out of the cargo bay as soon as the door came off.

The cargo bay, of course, had depressurized in the absence of the cabin door, and the suction of the depressurization of the bay caused the floor of the passenger cabin above to collapse, depressurizing the passenger cabin and breaking the cables that steered the rudder of the plane, causing the pilot to lose control.

But why had the door come off? The NTSB conducted tests and discovered that the DC-10 cargo door, when closed, could withstand 6,000 pounds (2,700 kg) of pressure, so it was unlikely that it had been forced open from inside. However, in another test, they made the surprising discovery that it was possible to latch the cabin door without completely closing it. Thus, the explanation for the accident was that the door had been improperly closed by a cargo handler at the airport and had been blown off by the pressure of the air inside the cargo bay.

The problem was, all DC-10s had defective doors like the one on the American jet.

The NTSB sent a list of strongly worded recommendations to the FAA, describing the danger the defective cargo doors presented to all passengers on DC-10 flights. They recommended that the cargo door on *all* DC-10s be replaced immediately, in order to minimize the chance of another such incident. Further, vents should be placed in the cargo bay to release air pressure in the event of sudden decompression, so that the floor of the passenger cabin would not be likely to collapse again.

At least one branch of the FAA, the Los Angeles Office, agreed fully with the NTSB and recommended that an Airworthiness Directive be issued, effectively ground-

A cargo door that was not properly closed caused
the crash of this Turkish Airlines DC-10 on
March 3, 1974. All 346 people aboard were killed.

ing all DC-10s until the modifications could be made. Of course, this would present an inconvenience to those airlines whose DC-10s represented a substantial portion of their fleet, and would deal a substantial public relations blow to the airplane's manufacturer, McDonnell-Douglas, but given the severity of the situation, and the possibility of the loss of human life, it would certainly be worthwhile.

The administrator of the FAA, J.H. Shaffer, did not agree. The situation, he apparently felt, was not as serious as the NTSB made it sound. Instead, he came to a "gentleman's agreement" with the chairman of Mc-Donnell-Douglas, who arranged for small windows to be inserted on the cargo doors so that baggage handlers could see if they were properly closed or not. Next to the windows were placed instructions, so that the cargo handler could read how to operate this rather unusual door arrangement.

The instructions, however, were written in English. Not all cargo handlers—and especially not those outside of the English-speaking world—could read the instructions.

And it was still possible to latch the door without fully closing it.

On March 3. 1974, a Turkish Airlines DC-10 left Orly International Airport in Paris on its way to London. Though no one on board was aware of it, the cargo door was not properly closed. When the airplane reached 13,000 feet (3,962 m), sufficient pressure built up in the cargo bay to blow it open.

Once again, the floor of the passenger cabin collapsed, and the cabin depressurized. The Captain, Nejat Berkoz, lost control of his airplane.

This time, however, no one succeeded in wrestling the craft back under control and flying back to the airport. Captain Berkoz's last words were: "I think we're going to hit the ground." And then: "Oops."

The plane sank rapidly into the Ermenonville Forest, outside of Paris. It exploded when it hit the ground. Three hundred and forty-six people died. It was, and remained for some years, the worst single-plane accident in aviation history.

Three days later, the Airworthiness Directive went out from the FAA. All cargo doors on DC-10 airplanes were to be modified. Immediately.

However, the damage had already been done, both to the aviation community and the reputation of the FAA. Even before the FAA could issue its AD, a special subcommittee of the House of Representatives began to investigate the agency. In January of 1975, it had this to say in a report entitled "Air Safety: a Selected Review of FAA Performance":

The subcommittee found throughout its inquiry—from the DC-10 crash to its most recent investigation into the feasibility of requiring Ground Proximity Warning Systems—a tendency for the agency to avoid the role of leadership in advancing air safety which the Congress intended it to assume. This is manifested primarily by the FAA's willingness to let the industry engage in self-regulation when vital safety measures are concerned. In some instances, this abdication of responsibility has been coupled with an administrative lethargy—a sluggishness which at times approaches an attitude of indifference to public safety. This must stop.

In short, the FAA is too soft on the airline industry, and not especially interested in air safety. Harsh words indeed.

Almost certainly the FAA learned a lesson in the DC-10 cargo door incident, because the next time the DC-10 had major problems—and indeed the DC-10 has had more than its share—the agency acted decisively. And, as it turned out, it was a good thing they did.

It was five years before the next major incident involving a DC-10. And while it was not quite as terrible a crash as the one in Paris in 1974, it remains to this day the worst single plane accident to take place in the United States.

American flight 191 left O'Hare Airport in Chicago at 3:00 P.M. on May 25, 1979—the start of the Memorial Day weekend. Just as the DC-10 lifted from the field, an engine came loose and struck the wing, destroying the slats on the left wing. Without the slats, the left wing did not produce sufficient lift at takeoff speed, and it stalled. The DC-10 rolled over and crashed. All 270 persons on board were killed.

In a sense, however, the real horror was just beginning. The FAA grounded the entire fleet of DC-10s in the United States, until they could be inspected. When they were inspected, a shocking fact was discovered: half of them, sixty-eight planes, were in sufficiently bad condition that they could not be allowed to fly until they had undergone repairs.

Why did this happen? How had it come about? How did these airplanes pass the periodic inspections through which the airlines and manufacturers were supposedly putting them? Was the DC-10 an inherently flawed airplane?

Some critics argued that it was, that McDonnell-Douglas had rushed it into production in the early 1970s to compete with Boeing and Lockheed.

But other critics cited deficiencies in the FAA certification process, implying that the agency was too willing to leave testing to the discretion of the manufacturers.

In 1985, several incidents have occurred involving structural failures on airliners, but none of them involving DC-10s.

In Manchester, England, on August 22, 1985, fifty-five people were killed in a British Airtours Boeing 737. The craft was accelerating down the runway at about 100 miles (160 km) an hour when an engine caught fire. The pilot immediately brought the airplane to a stop. However, suffocating smoke spread rapidly through the cabin; in a scene of wild panic most of the passengers managed to escape. The rest died in the smoke and flame, unable to get to a door.

What happened? The engine, a Pratt and Whitney JT8D, apparently fell apart; the engine chamber may have been faulty.

Barely more than two weeks later, on September 6, a Midwest Express DC-9 suffered an engine failure on its way out of Milwaukee Airport and stalled in the air. It plummeted to earth, killing all thirty-one persons on board. The engines on the DC-9 were also Pratt and Whitney JT8Ds. Although there is no indication that these crashes are connected in any fashion, there has nonetheless been concern about the airworthiness of the JT8D engine. The Pratt and Whitney Company has been quick to point out that more than 13,000 of the engines have been sold—in fact, it is the engine used in two-thirds of the commercial jets in the United States—and it has had an excellent safety record until now. On the basis of these two accidents, the FAA has not as of this writing found an airworthiness directive to be called for.

Perhaps the most frightening of all recent structural failures are those involving bombs that have exploded on airplanes. On June 23, 1985, an Air India Boeing 747 fell into the ocean off the coast of Ireland, killing all 329 people aboard. Although the official cause of the crash is, as of this writing, "unknown," two Indian terrorist groups have been implicated by anonymous sources as having planted bombs on the plane. Almost simultaneously with the crash of the Air India jet, a bomb exploded at New Tokyo International Airport, killing two workers. The baggage containing the bomb had just been unloaded from a plane.

The common thread in the two incidents is that both airplanes had recently taken on luggage at an airport in

Vancouver, British Columbia. The evidence, largely circumstantial in the case of the Air India jet, is that bombs had been smuggled aboard both planes at the Canadian airport, in luggage, probably by the same militant terrorist group. The Canadian prime minister insisted that the security at his country's airports was "the most stringent in the world" but promised that nonetheless he would put that security system under intense scrutiny.

Further evidence in the Air India case lies deep below the waters off the Irish coast, though underwater salvage robots have already been used to extract the black-box recorders from the airplane. Unfortunately, the recorders had stopped moments before the crash had occurred, perhaps because the electrical system powering the recorders had stopped functioning when the hypothetical bomb exploded. More of the airplane must be retrieved before it can be determined whether the craft was downed by a bomb, and this will be a formidable task indeed.

Bombings are a situation that no airplane manufacturer can anticipate in airplane design. We can only hope that security measures can be taken to prevent such incidents from happening in the future.

CHAPTER FOUR
RIDERS ON THE STORM

For Washington, D.C., January 13 was almost certainly the worst day of the winter of 1982—and arguably one of the worst days the city will ever see. A heavy snow had begun falling during the early afternoon, and by 4:00 P.M. the streets were clogged with automobiles driven by government workers who had taken off early to beat the rush-hour traffic. On the Fourteenth Street Bridge, spanning the now icy Potomac River to connect downtown Washington with the Virginia suburbs, cars were packed bumper to bumper.

Just across the river, at Washington National Airport, an Air Florida Boeing 737 sat on the runway, awaiting clearance for takeoff. The pilot, Larry Wheaton, regarded the snow with annoyance; he was already running forty-five minutes late. Finally, he received his go-ahead from the controllers in the tower. The 737 taxied down the runway, lifted its wheels into the air—and refused to go any higher.

Weighed down as though by some mysterious force, the plane sank back toward the ground—or, rather, toward the Potomac River, over which departing airplanes were directed to fly. Struggling to gain lift, the front end of the 737 strained toward the sky, but the tail end dragged far below. "Larry, we're going down, Larry," cried the copilot of the jet. Replied the pilot: "I know it." As the airplane passed over the Fourteenth Street Bridge, the tail struck the cement and smashed into a row of cars, killing four motorists. The airplane broke in two. The tail section rolled off the bridge and onto the ice below, where it remained afloat. The bulk of the plane continued on into the river, smashing through the ice and sinking into the freezing waters of the Potomac.

The passengers and crew in the front section were killed on impact, but four passengers and a flight attendant struggled out of the tail section and into the chilling water. A rescue helicopter, with the assistance of at least one heroic bystander, plucked the survivors from the river. The five people lived, but the other seventy-four people aboard died.

Ironically, the crash occurred within blocks of the National Transportation Safety Board's main office, but several members of the Go Team were stuck in traffic and were unable to reach the site. New members were assigned, and at least one arrived at the accident location on foot. Although the plane was still visible beneath the water, the icy conditions made it so difficult to reach the wreckage that it was nearly two weeks before the black-box recorder could be retrieved. The NTSB's verdict: ice on the wings; and ice on the engine probes, causing erroneous cockpit indications.

The Air Florida jet had undergone standard de-icing procedures while awaiting clearance for takeoff, but had been allowed to remain on the field for long moments after the de-icing was complete, while ice built up once again. The ice effectively altered the aerodynamic characteristics of the plane and added to its weight, and the 737 was unable to achieve lift. The result, of course, was disaster.

Weather, man's age-old nemesis. Weather-related disasters are nothing new; they are probably far older than the human race. But there is something especially poignant, and not a little nightmarish, about the image of a planeload of human beings fighting the elements while struggling to stay in the sky.

In some ways, though, weather has become less of a problem as the technology of flight has advanced. Jets, for instance, can fly over most bad weather conditions, experiencing them only on takeoff and landing.

And the sophisticated instruments used to guide pilots to and from airports (which we will discuss in more detail in the next chapter), have almost made the term "visibility" meaningless; a good pilot can practically land, take off and fly a plane without looking out the window, relying on instruments alone.

But it may be the fact that modern airplanes can withstand relatively extreme weather conditions that makes those conditions dangerous, because it fosters a sense of overconfidence in some pilots. A pilot who doesn't have sufficient respect for weather is a pilot heading for a crash. The very capriciousness—changeability—of weather is what makes airplanes crash. The weather plays tricks on aviators—and some of those tricks are deadly. Perhaps the deadliest of all is wind shear.

What is wind shear? Technically, wind shear is any sudden change in wind speed or direction, but usually it is part of a meteorological phenomenon called a microburst, which can occur in the middle of a thunderstorm, when wind begins to blow straight downward out of a cloud. When such a wind strikes the ground, it spreads outward in all directions—this is the microburst. A pilot flying into a microburst will experience a strong headwind, but as the airplane passes the center of the microburst, the headwind will turn abruptly into a tailwind. The result is that the airspeed of the plane—the speed of the plane relative to the air around it—can be severely reduced in a few seconds, and there isn't much that the pilot can do about it.

You'll recall from the last chapter that the lift produced by an airplane is completely dependent on the plane's airspeed, not its ground speed . When caught in a microburst wind shear, a plane can lose its lift entirely and plunge directly toward the ground. If this happened at a high altitude, the pilot would have ample opportunity to rev up the engines and get the air speed back to normal. But microbursts always happen right next to the ground, where there isn't much room to fall. Further, because pilots are most likely to encounter wind shear while taking off or landing, the airspeed of the craft is usually fairly low to begin with, and the wind shear can effectively reduce it to stall speed.

In the twelve years ending in 1985, at least twelve airline accidents have been attributed to wind shear. A thirteenth accident, which was almost certainly caused by wind shear, occurred in Texas on August 2, 1985, though the final verdict on the cause of that accident had not yet been returned by the NTSB at the time this book was being written.

In that accident, a Lockheed L-1011 jumbo jet, flown by Delta Airlines, crashed on its way into Dallas–Fort Worth Airport, in the middle of a thunderstorm. The airplane hit the ground north of the runway, bounced across a highway, hitting at least two cars and killing one driver, struck a water tower, and finally exploded. The L-1011's tail section broke loose before the explosion and the occupants of the last ten rows of seats survived; the other 133 individuals on the craft were killed. (Ironically, all of the survivors were in the smoking section, possibly the

only occasion when smoking was ever beneficial to someone's health.)

Probably, the plane was forced to the ground by wind shear; the accident has the classic trademarks. Structural failure is unlikely as a cause, since the L-1011 has an excellent record, having been involved in only two other major accidents worldwide since it was introduced in the late 1960s.

There are tricks that a pilot can use to get out of a wind shear-induced dive, but they don't always work and they must be executed rapidly if they are to work at all; wind shear is a quick killer and the pilot must be quicker in order to survive. The best way to combat a wind shear is not to get caught in it, but that is easier said than done. Wind shear is invisible, and often the pilot is not aware of it until it is too late to avoid it. Pilots could choose not to fly in any thunderstorms, but the truth is that most such storms are quite navigable and wind shear precautions are usually not necessary. The trick is to figure out when they are necessary.

What is needed is an automatic wind shear detection system. And, in fact, such systems exist, though they are far from foolproof. One of these, the so-called low-level

Dr. Carol Roberts of the National Transportation Safety Board displays the cockpit voice recorder and the digital flight data recorder boxes recovered from the Delta Airlines jumbo jet that crashed on its way into Dallas–Fort Worth Airport in August 1985. Investigators hoped to obtain confirming evidence that the accident was caused primarily by wind shear, and abrupt change in wind speed or direction.

wind shear alert system, is already available at a number of airports, but it doesn't work terribly well. It consists of a number of wind gauges—usually five or eleven—scattered around the perimeter of an airfield with one sensor directly in the middle. If one or more of the perimeter sensors register a drastically different wind speed than the sensor in the middle of the field, a computer in the air traffic control center sounds a wind shear alert, and pilots are warned away. Unfortunately, a microburst can easily take place between a pair of sensors, without being registered by either. Thus, there is no guarantee that a microburst will be detected by the low-level system, and quite often they are not.

A better system exists. Called doppler radar, it uses a sophisticated radar system to measure wind speeds all around an airport and is therefore capable of detecting even the smallest of wind shears. However, the FAA argues that most airports are not ready yet for the doppler system, because it requires a trained (and expensive) meteorologist to interpret its output. A computer could be programmed to read the doppler information and sound a wind shear alert, much as computers now do in the low-level system. But programming a computer to read such a complex body of data is no small task, and the software does not yet exist to do the job.

When it does, wind shear crashes may become a thing of the past. Until then, passengers and pilots who must land or take off in a thunderstorm can only cross their fingers and hope for the best.

CHAPTER FIVE
NO MARGIN FOR ERROR

The pilot of the Boeing 747 waiting on the runway at Tenerife Airport in the Canary Islands on March 27, 1977 had not been given clearance to take off. And certainly no competent air traffic controller would have given the KLM Airlines jet such a clearance, since there was already a Pan Am 747 taxiing onto the runway, about to intersect the first airplane's path. Yet, perhaps as a result of a tragic misunderstanding, the KLM pilot began his takeoff without clearance. The misunderstanding was compounded by a heavy fog that had settled over the field, preventing the pilot from seeing the Pan Am jet in his path until it was too late. The KLM airplane had just lifted its wheels from the ground when the two craft collided.

The Pan Am jet was literally torn apart, and exploded violently into flame. The KLM 747 fell back to the runway and also exploded. Everyone on board the KLM jet died. Sixty-seven people managed to escape from the Pan Am craft, but 268 were killed. The tragic total: 583 dead. The worst aviation accident of all time.

What went wrong? Who can say? Recordings of the conversations between the traffic controllers in the airport tower show that no clearance was ever given to the KLM pilot, but imply that he may have thought that such clearance had been given. Whatever the reason, he flew his plane when he was not supposed to do so, and paid the price for his mistake.

Human error. Roughly 65 percent of all aviation accidents are put down to unfortunate mistakes. Someone acted when they weren't supposed to—or failed to act when they should have. Or just plain fouled up.

Pilots don't like to talk much about pilot error, because the subject reflects badly on their profession. When they do talk about it, they tend to use terms like "human error involvement in accidents," which politely obscure the subject under a cloud of ambiguity.

And, indeed, there is a lot of ambiguity on this subject. When a plane crashes in bad weather, for instance, is the weather the cause of the accident? Or is it the pilot's fault for flying into bad weather in the first place? The Air Florida accident described in the last chapter was obviously caused by ice. But the larger cause, as recognized by the accident investigators, was pilot error: the pilot should not have allowed his craft to fly under such conditions. Interestingly, the flight recorder transcript of conversations in the Air Florida cockpit just before takeoff indicates that the copilot was aware that something was wrong in his instrument readings, but failed to press the issue on the oblivious pilot:

> COPILOT: God, look at that thing.
> COPILOT: That don't seem right, does it?
> COPILOT: Ah, that's not right.
> PILOT: Yes, it is, there's 80.
> COPILOT: Naw, I don't think that's right.
> COPILOT: Ah, maybe it is.

Daunted by his failure to convince the pilot that something was wrong with the instrument readings, the copilot instead convinced himself that the readings were okay—a fatal error.

Some pilots honestly believe that the 65 percent error figure isn't entirely fair, that the airline industry insists on blaming pilots for accidents to avoid taking responsibility of its own. As one United Airlines pilot, quoted by *Newsweek* magazine, put it: "If they blame the problem on pilot error, they don't have to make changes."

Still, the problem of pilot error is a worrisome one, and the Airline Pilot's Association (ALPA) has joined hands with NASA's Ames Research Center to study factors that could lead to errors in the cockpit, such as fatigue and conflict between crew members.

The National Transportation Safety Board has also expressed an interest in the problem, and in 1983 began an active investigation of human errors in several types of transportation accidents, including those involving airplanes. The NTSB's Human Performance Division gathers and analyzes data relating to accidents involving human error and tries to determine why the accidents occurred, not just how.

In a sense, however, pilot error is less of a problem now than it was in the early days of aviation, simply because much of the process of flying is becoming automated—that is, it is being taken over by machines. And, as machines and computer systems become increasingly more sophisticated and as they become increasingly a part of the flying process, the chances of pilot error will grow smaller and smaller. Of course, critics of automation may argue in turn that the chances of computer error will grow proportionally greater. But, in an age of faster and larger jet planes, we have long ago passed the point where a human being can control all of the factors involved in safe flight; only computers are fast enough to monitor the constantly changing environment around the aircraft, and capable of performing the complex calculations involved without error.

One example of the way in which automation has become increasingly part of flight since its early days is the navigation systems used to guide pilots between airports.

The very first pilots navigated by the seat of their pants, verifying their positions by looking out the window of the airplane and flying in the direction where they knew their destination lay. This was not an entirely satisfactory system of navigation; what was the pilot to do in bad weather or in the dark of night? And, as planes flew faster and higher, even clear-weather flights could not always find their way across the United States by visual navigation alone.

Early on, seat-of-the-pants flying was augmented by the radio beams that we talked about in Chapter Two, which helped a pilot find his way across country by listening to the sound of the beam on his cockpit radio. Today, these radio beams have been replaced by the VORTAC navigation system.

VORTAC stands for very-high-frequency omnirange radio/tactical air navigation. VORTAC systems are available at most major airports. How does VORTAC work? A VORTAC navigation system broadcasts 360 separate radio beams, called radials, around an airport, in 360 different directions. (The older radio beams were only broadcast in four directions.) These beams are detected by VORTAC receivers on board airplanes. By spinning a dial on the VORTAC receiver and aligning a needle in the center of a gauge, a pilot can tell if he or she is flying directly toward an airport or away from it. Because the VORTAC system produces so many more beams than the older system, the pilot has a much larger choice of directions from which to approach the airport. And because the VORTAC receiver reports its information visually rather

The cockpit of today's jumbo jet, equipped with numerous dials, switches, lights, screens, and more to insure a safe flight.

than audibly, the signal is much less subject to disruption from various kinds of radio interference, such as lightning.

VORTAC makes the process of navigation almost automatic. And once the airplane arrives at the airport, the pilot can use a second automatic system, based at the airport, to help the airplane land: the instrument landing system, ILS for short, which guides the airplane gently and accurately to the ground.

Seat-of-the-pants flying isn't dead, of course; pilots of small planes do it all the time. A pilot who navigates by sight is said to be flying under visual flight rules, or VFR. A pilot who flies according to the automatic guidance of his or her instruments is said to be flying under instrument flight rules, or IFR. Although a properly trained pilot can always choose to fly IFR, there are certain conditions under which VFR flying is quite inappropriate: when visibility is obscured by a storm, for instance. Jet pilots always fly under IFR, because their craft fly too high and fast for visual navigation.

More sophisticated automatic equipment will be available in the near future, to further reduce the chances of pilot error. Perhaps the most significant of these are the automatic collision-avoidance systems. When such systems are in the cockpit of all commercial airplanes, midair collisions may become a thing of the past.

Interestingly, such systems have been available for years, but the FAA has never authorized any such systems for general installation. Why not? To answer that question, we'll have to look at how such a system would work.

An automatic collision-avoidance system would first need to recognize when two airplanes were sufficiently

A departing jet passes the control tower of LaGuardia Airport.

close together to present a problem. One way in which this could be done would be to place a computer system on each aircraft capable of "talking," via radio, with similar computer systems on other aircraft. The computers would compare information about the relative positions of their respective airplanes and decide if a collision might be imminent. If so, they would pass this information on to the pilot, probably through an amplified message piped into the cabin, along the lines of "Collision alert! Collision alert!" followed by information concerning the position of the intruding airplane. If prompt action needed to be taken to avoid the other craft, the computer could give specific instructions for evasive maneuvers: "Pull up! Pull up!" or "Dive! Dive!" Naturally, a problem would result if the pilots of both airplanes were told to pull up, or to dive; thus, the two computers would need to decide among themselves which plane should go up and which down, and relay the appropriate requests to the pilots.

Alternatively, the collision-avoidance computer could be based on the ground, probably in an air traffic control center. It could receive information from transponderlike devices (see Chapter Two) on board all of the aircraft in its vicinity and use that information—which would include position, speed, and altitude data—to decide if any two craft were coming perilously close to one another. It could then broadcast emergency information to the appropriate planes.

The problem with such collision-avoidance systems is that they must be absolutely trustworthy; they must never broadcast false collision alerts or inappropriate evasive maneuvers. An airplane that dived to avoid a collision, for instance, might endanger craft flying at a lower level; hence, such a maneuver should only be taken if absolutely necessary. And a pilot must be able to respond instantly when the collision alert sounds; there is no time to verify that a collision is actually about to take place.

Although most collision-avoidance systems are trustworthy in collision situations encountered between airports, they become more erratic when an airplane is about to land, or take off, at an airport. The proximity of so many nearby craft tends to trigger the collision-avoidance warning, even though the nearby planes usually represent no immediate threat. Hence, a pilot might well be tempted to turn the system off altogether when approaching or leaving an airport; yet, this is the point where it is probably needed the most. The last midair collision in the United States, for instance, occurred over San Diego Airport (see Chapter Two), and could have been avoided by a good collision-avoidance system.

Finally, whatever is chosen as the standard system will need to be placed on all airplanes, not just some, since most such systems involve the computerized comparison of information from the two airplanes to determine their relative positions. Hence, it will need to be inexpensive, so that even the owners of small private planes can install them. Yet, some of the systems under consideration cost over 50,000 dollars apiece, which places them well outside the budget of most part-time pilots.

The ideal collision-avoidance system may not exist yet, but the FAA has promised that some such system will be required as part of the National Airspace System, which we discussed in Chapter Two.

CHAPTER SIX
HOW TO SURVIVE

After reading the last five chapters, you may have decided never to take another airplane trip in your life.

Relax. As we said at the beginning, flying is safe. More than a million people take airplane trips every day, and in most years far less than 1,000 of them are killed. That's roughly one passenger out of 400,000. The odds are in your favor.

But suppose that, against all reasonable odds, you do find yourself in an airplane crash. Is there anything you can do to increase your chances of coming out alive?

Well, if your airplane collides with another airplane several miles in the air, or plows into the side of a mountain at full throttle, nothing short of prayer is likely to do you any good. The aviation community terms such crashes as nonsurvivable accidents, because nobody walks away from them alive, except by an occasional whim of fate.

However, nonsurvivable accidents are a rarity. They don't happen very often. Most accidents are survivable accidents, which is to say that they involve either no collision or a very mild collision, and most passengers are still alive and in one piece when the airplane comes to a stop.

Strangely, a lot of people die in this kind of accident, too. Here's an example:

In September 1983, a DC-10 was taxiing down the the runway at the Malaga Airport, in Spain, when the pilot heard an unexplained noise. Thinking that something might be wrong with his craft, he canceled the takeoff and braked the airplane to a halt. Unfortunately, the DC-10 could not be stopped in time; it continued off the edge of the airstrip, ran through a fence, and came to rest in an open field.

There was no crash; some of the passengers in the forward section of the cabin were barely jostled as the DC-10 rolled to a stop, though apparently damage did occur to seats in the rear. But one of the wings had struck an obstacle and was knocked loose from the airplane. Apparently the tail of the plane struck the detached wing, because the tail section of the DC-10 caught fire.

Passengers in the rear, prevented from going forward by damaged seats blocking the aisle, tried to escape through the two rear doors—but the doors would not open. Within five minutes, fifty people in the rear of the plane died of smoke inhalation.

And yet, according to the NTSB investigation of the accident, a second unblocked aisle was available to allow these passengers to reach the open exits in the front of the airplane. Why had they not used this aisle? No one knows. Had these passengers listened to the evacuation briefing given by the stewardess at the beginning of the flight? Had they read the cards available at each seat explaining how to escape from the airplane in the event of an emergency? According to the NTSB 1983 Annual Report:

When survivors were interviewed, many indicated that their evacuation had not been influenced either by what they had been told in the evacuation briefing, or by what they had read on the seat back card. In fact, many of the survivors indicated that they had not read the seat back cards, nor could they recall the oral briefing.

It's not hard to imagine what went through the minds of the fire victims as they attempted to escape through the locked exits at the rear of the DC-10: nothing at all. Without any knowledge of what was to be done in the event of a crash, they panicked and headed mindlessly in the same direction as everyone else. Probably, they didn't even realize that the door they were heading for was locked.

Something similar happened in the explosion of the British Airtours 737 described in Chapter Three. Panicky passengers fought one another to reach the exit—and only some escaped. One survivor, quoted in the *Washington Post*, said: "It was crazy in there. You looked after yourself with no thought for anyone else at all. . . . If we hadn't panicked, more people would have got out."

The first rule of escaping from an airline accident, then, is: Don't panic.

That's easier said than done, of course, especially when all the people around you are losing their heads. Still, the great antidote for panic is knowledge; if you understand a few things about surviving an accident, you are less likely to panic when an emergency arises. Hence, here is a quick primer on surviving a "survivable crash":

According to National Transportation Safety Board figures, more than 90 percent of airplane accidents involve fires. Airplane fuel is highly flammable, and even a fire that begins outside the craft can spread to the inside in one or two minutes. You do not want to be trapped inside the plane when this happens.

Hence, you should always be aware of where the nearest exit is located, so that you can get to it quickly once the airplane is on the ground. In fact, you should be aware of where several exits are located and how to reach them, because there is a chance that the exit nearest you could be damaged in the crash, or be inaccessible for some other reason. If you can't figure out where the exits are, ask a flight attendant—but don't wait until after an accident occurs! Then, the flight attendants will have their hands full and won't have time to answer individual questions. Of course, if there is an accident, it is the job of the flight attendants to direct all passengers to the nearest exits, but if the flight attendants are incapacitated during the accident, you'll be on your own. And if your fellow passengers should panic, there won't be much that the flight attendant can do to prevent a stampede.

Knowing where the exit is will not necessarily be all the information you need to get through it. You may have to open it, particularly if you are the first to get there. Exit doors are not necessarily easy to open. Many come with instructions attached, but you won't have time to read them while the airplane is being evacuated. You might not even be able to read them; there may be no light in the cabin or the cabin may be filled with smoke. If you have the opportunity, read the instructions before the airplane takes off, so that you will know how to open the door if the occasion should arise.

Most exits fall into two categories: large doors of the sort that you use when you enter and leave the plane at the airport, and emergency exits, which are placed next to selected seats in the cabin and may resemble the ordinary windows found next to other seats, except that they should have signs above or next to them identifying them as exits. A typical passenger airplane may have only one or two of the first kind of exit, but several of the second kind. If all goes well, a flight attendant should open the main door or doors to the plane, but opening an emergency exit is often the responsibility of the passenger sitting next to it.

To open an emergency exit, you must first find the handle and then pull it. The handle may have a cover over it which you must first remove. When you find the handle, pull it down, and pull the exit door out of the wall. You may then use the exit—but check first to see if it is safe to do so. Most emergency exits let out onto the wing, but after a crash the wing may be on fire—or not there at all. Exits that do not let out onto the wing may have ropes attached that you can use to lower yourself to the ground. First, however, you must pull the rope out of its receptacle.

If you use a main door instead of an emergency exit, you may have to go down an escape slide to reach the ground. This is an inflatable tube with a slick surface that you can use to slide more or less safely to the ground below—more or less because, in some accidents, more passengers are injured tumbling off the slide than in the crash itself. Nonetheless the slide is a fast way to get out, and you will probably be grateful to find it there. The slide should drop down automatically when the door is opened.

The above assumes that your airplane has come to rest on land; if you should have to bail out in the middle of the ocean, you will need to take extra precautions.

Any airplane that flies more than 50 miles (80 km) from land must carry with it life jackets for the passengers. In some cases you will find these life jackets underneath your seat; however, other airplanes may stow the jackets

Employees at Boeing testing an evacuation chute for their 747, in response to Federal Aviation Administration requirements.

elsewhere. A flight attendant will probably give you this information before the flight; if not, don't be afraid to ask.

On many airplanes, the seat cushions double as flotation devices; take these cushions with you when you leave the plane and lie atop them to stay afloat in the water. However, not all seat cushions serve a double purpose; make sure to find out in advance if yours do.

If you must evacuate an airplane on land or sea, there is one rule that you should always follow: don't carry any luggage with you. It doesn't matter if everything you own is stored in the suitcase in the baggage rack, or the knapsack under your feet: leave it on the plane! If possible you can retrieve it later, but it isn't worth risking your life to get it out. For one thing, you don't have the time to grab anything; for another, carrying baggage can endanger the safety of other passengers—if it flies out of your hands as you go down the escape slide, for instance.

Fire will greatly complicate your ability to get to an exit. For one thing, fires produce smoke—and smoke is deadly and blinding. Don't breathe the smoke if at all possible; it necessary, bend down to get under it. Fortunately, smoke tends to rise, and you may have room to maneuver beneath it. However, the presence of smoke makes it more imperative than ever that you know where the exit is, because you will not be able to see it if you are crawling on the floor, in the dark. If you see fire, go the other way—unless there is absolutely no alternative, And don't waste any time getting out of the plane; fire moves fast, usually a lot faster than you imagine it will.

The above is just a short, beginning lesson on air crash survival. To find out more, you might want to read the book *Just in Case*, by Daniel A. Johnson, mentioned in the bibliography at the end of this book. And be sure to listen to the speech the flight attendant gives at the beginning of your flight, and read the card in the pouch on the back of the seat in front of you that tells you what to do in case of an emergency.

And if you have finished this chapter more frightened of flying than ever, just bear in mind that it is very unlikely that you will ever need the advice provided by the above paragraphs. But if the unlikely comes to pass, you'll be glad that you know what to do. Very glad indeed.

CHAPTER SEVEN
HOW SAFE IS IT ... REALLY?

So just how safe is commercial flying?

Let's look at some statistics.

For every 1 billion passenger miles—that is, for every one passenger carried 1 billion miles or every billion passengers carried 1 mile—one person is killed in an accident involving a scheduled airline.

By contrast, 10.6 people are killed in automobile accidents per 1 billion passenger miles. Hence, flying airplanes is about ten times safer than riding in a car or taking a taxi.

On the other hand, there are safer ways to travel. Only 0.8 people are killed in railroad accidents per billion passenger miles and only 0.4 people in bus accidents.

Still, flying in a plane isn't all that dangerous.

But, as we said at the beginning of this book, the real question may not be "Is flying safe?" but "Is it safe enough?"

Is it in our power to make flying safer?

Yes, it is, say the experts. We've already seen some

of the ways that flying could be made safer: Doppler radar to detect wind shear, collision-avoidance systems to avoid midair collisions. But there are other ways in which the safety of flying could be improved as well. Let's take a look at some of them.

In a survivable accident, as described in the last chapter, the greatest enemy is fire. If it were possible to minimize the danger from fire, a much larger number of passengers could survive.

Since it is usually the airplane fuel that catches fire, one way to decrease the chances of fire after an accident would be to use a fuel that does not burn.

This isn't as easy as it sounds, though, because the ability to burn is desirable in a fuel; controlled burning is the way in which the fuel generates the energy that runs the engine. Thus, the problem is to devise a fuel that will burn when it is in the engine—where it is supposed to burn—but not while it is in the tank.

One way to achieve this end is to add a substance called antimisting compound, or AMK, to the fuel. AMK, which was developed for the FAA and NASA (the National Aeronautics and Space Administration) by British and American chemical companies, is a fuel additive that causes fuel to drip out of a tank in large gobs rather than spraying out in a fine mist. Because the gobs of fuel have less oxygen in them than the mist, they are less likely to burn, because oxygen is necessary for fire. When the AMK-treated fuel enters the jet engine, on the other hand, a mechanical device called a degrader breaks up the gobs so that the fuel can burn.

In theory, adding such a substance to airplane fuel is the answer to the problem of nonsurvivable "survivable" crashes; in practice, the concept needs a little work. In December of 1984, the FAA and NASA deliberately crashed an unoccupied Boeing 720 jetliner on a field at Edwards Air Force Base in California to see if they could prevent a postcollision fire by treating the fuel with AMK.

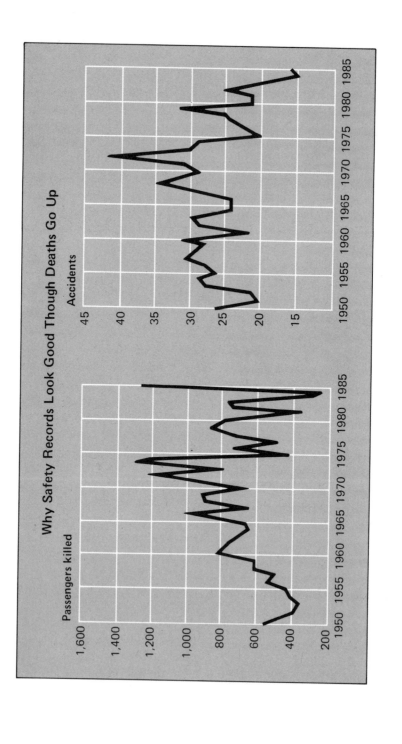

Why Safety Records Look Good Though Deaths Go Up

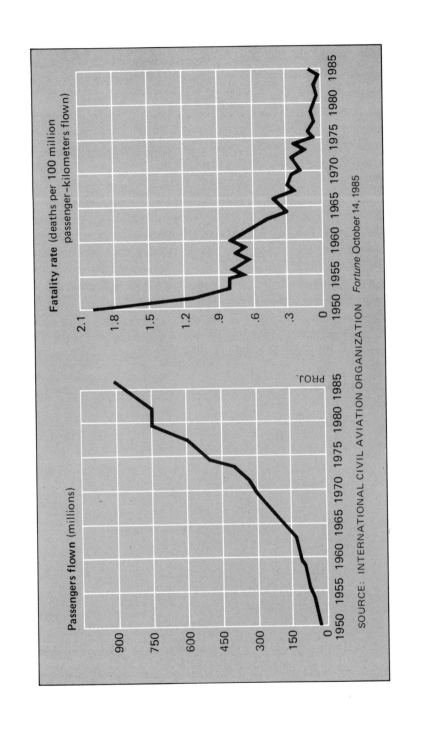

Passengers flown (millions)

900
750
600
450
300
150
0

1950 1955 1960 1965 1970 1975 1980 1985

PROJ.

Fatality rate (deaths per 100 million passenger–kilometers flown)

2.1
1.8
1.5
1.2
.9
.6
.3
0

1950 1955 1960 1965 1970 1975 1980 1985

SOURCE: INTERNATIONAL CIVIL AVIATION ORGANIZATION   *Fortune* October 14, 1985

The result: the plane erupted into flame. The antimisting compound did not work.

What went wrong? No one is quite sure. But work on flame retardants such as AMK is sure to continue.

In a 1982 report, the National Transportation Safety Board suggested that, during the period from 1970 to 1981, roughly 1,850 people lost their lives due to inadequacies of the interior design of airplanes. "Many deaths and injuries," the board said, "are directly attributable to failures of seats and cabin furnishings."

One problem associated with the interior design of airplanes is collapsing seats. Under the force of a collision, airline seats can become detached from the floor, and can be flung against the front of the cabin. The result is that a row of seats can collapse like an accordion, trapping and even crushing passengers. When seats come loose in the rear of a cabin, they present a danger to all passengers in the front of the cabin—and such seat collapses can happen even in a relatively minor survivable crash.

The solution is to find seats, and methods of anchoring seats, that can withstand the forces of an airplane crash—but that is easier said than done. For one thing, there is substantial argument over the best way to test the strength of seats, short of actually crashing a plane.

Critics of the FAA argue that they have been inexcusably slow in requiring effective seat attachments on commercial airlines.

There is also some argument among safety experts as to the way in which seats should be arranged in an aircraft. Although it is traditional, and not entirely illogical, to place the seats so that they face forward, there is a school of thought that says it is safer for the seats to face backward, toward the rear of the plane, as seats do on Air Force transport planes.

The idea of the aft-facing seat is that during a crash a passenger will be thrown into the seat rather than out of it, thus making it less likely that the passenger will be tossed into the aisle or into the next seat. However, there is some evidence that aft-facing seats collapse even more readily than forward-facing seats, increasing the possibility of passengers becoming trapped in their seats when they should be evacuating the plane. And there is reason to believe that passengers would resent being asked to ride backwards in a plane, just as they would rather not ride backwards in a car.

A long-standing argument between the NTSB and the FAA concerns the FAA's standards for safety belts on airplane seats. The FAA requires that safety belts be able to withstand a crash force of 9 G's (that is, a force equal to nine times the force of gravity on the surface of the earth). And yet the standard for safety belts in automobiles says that they must withstand a crash force of 25 G's! Why should automobiles be subject to stricter crash standards than airplanes?

The arguments about safety standards on aircraft will probably continue as long as there is an aviation industry, which will be as long as the human race endures. Perhaps air travel will never be as safe as it could be, but that may only be because human beings will not be satisfied with anything less than 100 percent safety, which may not be achievable.

Though 1985 was a particularly bad year for aviation safety, this was probably only a statistical anomaly, a run of bad luck. There was no common thread to the accidents of that year, no indication that a single overriding safety problem has gotten out of hand and threatens everyone who flies. And, in fact, the previous year, 1984, was one of the safest in aviation history, with only 224 passengers killed worldwide.

The truth is, commercial aviation is remarkably safe.

The very fact that we can climb into a jumbo jet on one side of the United States, and fly with an almost, if not quite, total guarantee of physical safety to the opposite side of the country—an act that would have been unthinkable far less than a century ago—is nothing short of incredible.

We should never grow complacent about air safety—standards should always be improved, and certainly never allowed to degenerate—but we can be proud of the standards that we have already achieved. The horror stories in this book are reminders that aviation is not completely free of danger—but then, what is?

CHRONOLOGY OF AIR SAFETY

1903—The first airplane flight in history; at Kitty Hawk, North Carolina, on December 17.

1907—The first fatal airplane crash in history. The pilot: Orville Wright, co-inventor of the airplane. The victim: Army Lieutenant Thomas E. Selfridge.

1914–1918—World War I, the first war in which airplanes played a significant role. Flight technology was greatly accelerated by the war, and a generation of pilots learned how to fly, though not necessarily safely, in the skies above Europe.

The 1920s—Age of the barnstormers, air mail pilots, and first passenger airlines. The infancy of modern aviation.

The 1930s—The decade in which modern aviation came into its own. The three major aircraft manufacturers—Boeing, McDonnell-Douglas, and Lockheed—made their first impact during this decade, and Douglas introduced what was quite possibly the most popular airplane of all time, the DC-3.

1935—Pilot Harvey Bolton, on the stormy night of May 5, accidentally pilots his DC-2 into a ravine, killing himself and four others, including U.S. Senator Bronson Cutting. Known as the "Cutting Crash," this incident brought about legislation that led eventually to the modern air safety system.

1938—The Civil Aeronautics Act is passed by Congress, establishing the Civil Aeronautics Administration (CAA) and the Civil Aeronautics Board (CAB), which later gave way to the Federal Aviation Administration (FAA) and the National Transportation Safety Board (NTSB).

The 1940s—Radar, developed during World War II, is introduced to air traffic control, allowing controllers to monitor the precise movements of aircraft around airports (and, later, between airports).

The 1950s—Jet airplanes are introduced to commercial aviation, greatly increasing the possibility of hazardous midair collisions.

1956—The first midair collision, over the Grand Canyon, between a TWA Super-Constellation and a United Airlines DC-7, on June 30.

1960—The first midair collision involving a jet, over New York City, on December 16.

The 1960s—Jumbo jets are introduced to commercial aviation, greatly increasing the number of passengers that can be carried on a single plane and, alas, the number that can die or be injured in a single crash.

1977—a KLM Airlines Boeing 747 collides with a Pan American Airlines 747 at Tenerife Airport in the Canary Islands, killing 583 people in the worst aviation accident of all time.

1979—American flight 191 crashes on takeoff at O'Hare Airport in Chicago, the worst single-plane accident to take place in the United States.

1981—The Professional Air Traffic Controller's Organization (PATCO) goes on strike, leading to the firing of most of the nation's air traffic controllers by President Ronald Reagan.

1985—Japan Air Lines flight 123 crashes into Mount Osutaka in Japan on August 12, killing 520 people—the worst single-plane disaster in aviation history.

The 1980s and 1990s—The introduction of the National Airspace System, which will supposedly modernize air traffic control, primarily through the increased use of computers in monitoring and controlling aircraft flight patterns.

FOR FURTHER READING

Artwick, Bruce, et al. *Flight Simulator II.* Champaign, Ill. : SubLogic Corporation, 1984.

A computer program available for Commodore 64, Atari 800, IBM, and Apple II series microcomputers. An excellent introduction to IFR and VFR flight, with a detailed simulation of VORTAC navigation.

Biggs, Don. *Pressure Cooker.* New York: W. W. Norton, 1979.

A detailed look at the job of the air traffic controller, written before the PATCO strike.

Johnson, Daniel A. *Just in Case: A Passenger's Guide to Airplane Safety and Survival.* New York: Plenum Press, 1984.

An excellent manual on crash survival, by an aviation safety expert.

Knauth, Percy. *Safety in the Skies.* Blue Ridge Summit, Pa. : TAB Books, 1982.

A readable history of aviation safety, with a special emphasis on air traffic control.

Solberg, Carl. *Conquest of the Skies: A History of Commercial Aviation in America.* Boston: Little, Brown, 1979.
A detailed, entertaining account of the aviation industry in the United States, from the Wright brothers to the present.

Varley, John. *Millennium.* New York: Berkley Books, 1983.
Probably the only science fiction novel ever written about the National Transportation Safety Board; lively, well written, and filled with interesting, if outlandish, speculation about what really goes on during a nonsurvivable crash.

INDEX

9842

BLAIRSVILLE SENIOR HIGH SCHOOL
BLAIRSVILLE, PENNA.